# Clyde Tombaugh

## and the Search for Planet X

by Margaret K. Wetterer
illustrations by Laurie A. Caple

Carolrhoda Books, Inc./Minneapolis

*For Charlie and our grandchildren*—M.K.W.

*For my grandmother and shining star, Elizabeth Ohmen*
—L.A.C.

I want to express my heartfelt appreciation to Clyde W. Tombaugh,
who answered all my letter queries so promptly and thoroughly
and who generously read and commented on the manuscript.
—M.K.W.

The publisher wishes to thank the following people for their assistance in the
preparation of this book: Capt. Charles J. Wetterer, Director of the U.S. Air Force
Academy Observatory; Helen Horstman, of the Lowell Observatory; and Dr. Henry
Giclas, Clyde W. Tombaugh's friend and associate at the Lowell Observatory.

Pronunciation note: The name Tombaugh is pronounced TAHM-baw.

Text copyright © 1996 by Carolrhoda Books, Inc.
Illustrations copyright © 1996 by Laurie A. Caple
The photograph on page 47 appears courtesy of the Lowell Observatory.

*This book is available in two editions:*
Library binding by Carolrhoda Books, Inc., a division of Lerner Publishing Group
Soft cover by First Avenue Editions, an imprint of Lerner Publishing Group
241 First Avenue North, Minneapolis, MN 55401 U.S.A.

Website address: www.lernerbooks.com

Library of Congress Cataloging-in-Publication Data

Wetterer, Margaret K.
    Clyde Tombaugh and the search for planet X / by Margaret K. Wetterer ;
illustrations by Laurie A. Caple.
        p.   cm. — (Carolrhoda on my own books)
    Summary:  The story of the young farm boy who became an astronomer
and discovered the planet Pluto at the age of twenty-four.
    ISBN 0-87614-893-3 (lib. bdg. : alk. paper)
    ISBN 0-87614-969-7 (pbk. : alk. paper)
    1. Tombaugh, Clyde William, 1906–1997    Biography—Juvenile literature.
2. Pluto (Planet)—Juvenile literature. 3. Astronomers—United States—
Biography—Juvenile literature. [1. Tombaugh, Clyde William, 1906–1997
2. Astronomers. 3. Pluto (Planet)] I. Caple, Laurie A., ill. II. Title.
III. Series: Carolrhoda on my own book.
QB36.T6W48   1996
520'.92—dc20
[B]                                                                    96-2056

Manufactured in the United States of America
3  4  5  6  7  8  –  JR  –  07  06  05  04  03  02

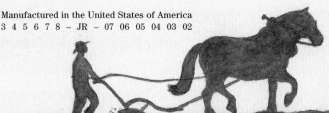

## Author's Note

Since ancient times, people have known of the five "wandering stars": Mercury, Venus, Mars, Jupiter, and Saturn. Sky watchers observed them as they moved through the background of "fixed stars." With the invention of the telescope in the early 1600s, astronomers learned the true nature of these wanderers: They were planets, like the earth itself, orbiting around the sun.

In 1781, William Herschel used a telescope to discover a seventh planet, Uranus. Astronomers soon saw that Uranus did not move exactly in its predicted path around the sun. The gravity of another, more distant planet must be pulling on Uranus. Astronomers figured out mathematically where this unseen planet might be. In 1846, an eighth planet, Neptune, was discovered.

Still, the paths of Uranus and Neptune seemed to be affected by something else.

Could it be the pull of an even more distant planet?

*Streator, Illinois*
*August 1918*

The full moon was shining brightly.

The summer night was warm.

Uncle Lee had set up

his small telescope

in a field behind his house.

Twelve-year-old Clyde waited
while his mother and father looked
at the night sky through the telescope.
Although Clyde had never looked
through a telescope before,
he knew it would make faraway things
look bigger and closer.

Finally, it was Clyde's turn.
Uncle Lee pointed the telescope
at the moon,
and Clyde looked.
He was amazed to see
mountains and craters,
plains and valleys.
Before, the moon had been
just an object in the sky.

Now Clyde could see that the moon
was really another world.
What other mysteries
were out there in space?
Clyde wondered.
Long after his parents
had lost interest,
Clyde and Uncle Lee gazed
through the telescope and
talked about the planets and stars.

Uncle Lee lent Clyde
a book on astronomy,
the study of the planets and stars.
Clyde read and re-read the book
until he almost knew it by heart.
Then he read every other
astronomy book he could find.
Soon Clyde could pick out
the constellations,
or groups of stars.

He learned to find the five planets
that could be seen
without a telescope:
Mercury, Venus, Mars,
Jupiter, and Saturn.
Clyde pointed out the stars and planets
to his younger brothers and sister.
After a while, Clyde's father
and Uncle Lee bought a new telescope
to share.

When Clyde was sixteen,
his family moved from Illinois
to a farm in Kansas.
Uncle Lee let Clyde take
the shared telescope with him.
There was much work to do
at the new farm.
Still, no matter how hard he worked
during the day,
Clyde always spent clear nights
studying the sky.
When he graduated from high school,
Clyde wanted to go to college
and become an astronomer.
But his family needed his help
on the farm.

So Clyde studied at home
in his free time.
He borrowed books on astronomy.
But what he really wanted was
a bigger, more powerful telescope.
Clyde didn't have the money to buy one,
so he decided to build it.

Clyde sent away for the things
he needed to build a telescope.
The most important part
was the mirror.
Unless the curve of the mirror
was just right,
the views through the telescope
would not be clear.

Clyde spent weeks
grinding and polishing
the glass for the mirror.
Again and again he tested its curve.
But when Clyde finally put
the mirror in his telescope,
the planets and stars looked blurry.
He would have to start over.

13

To make a good test
of the mirror's curve,
Clyde needed a place where
the temperature stayed the same
and the air was still.
So he asked his father
if they could build a cellar.

With just a pick and a shovel,
Clyde dug a huge pit.
Then some neighbors helped
Clyde and his father
finish the cellar.
The cool, still air of the new cellar
was the perfect place for Clyde
to shape and test his mirror.

Uncle Lee gave Clyde money
to build a telescope for him.
For weeks, Clyde ground and polished
and tested the mirror
in the new cellar.
Uncle Lee's telescope was excellent.
Then Clyde built a telescope
for himself.

With this telescope,
he could see many details
on the moon, Jupiter, Saturn, and Mars.
Clyde made drawings of what he saw.

Three years after high school,

Clyde was still working on the farm.

The farm was doing well.

Soon the oats would be

ready for harvest.

With the money the oats would bring,
Clyde could start college
and study to become an astronomer.
At last Clyde's dream
would come true.

But a few days later,
black clouds gathered.
The wind rose.
Rain poured down.
Suddenly, hail stones
pounded the oat field.
In just twenty minutes,
the storm was over.
All the oats were destroyed.
And so was Clyde's dream of college.

The storm made Clyde decide
to leave farming.
Even if he couldn't go to college,
he wanted to work in science.
He sent his best drawings
of Jupiter and Mars to
the Lowell Observatory in Arizona.
Maybe someone there could help him.

The letter Clyde received back
surprised him.
The observatory was looking
for someone to work
with their new camera telescope.
Dr. V. M. Slipher,
the director of the observatory,
offered Clyde a job.

On January 14, 1929,

Clyde set off

on the long train ride to Arizona.

He did not have enough money

for a bed on the train,

so he sat up the whole way.

When the train stopped

in a town so the passengers

could buy dinner,

Clyde ate the sandwiches

his mother had packed for him.

Clyde was both happy and nervous
about the great adventure
that lay ahead.
He was determined to be a success.
He had to be.
He did not have enough money
for a train ticket home.

*Lowell Observatory*
*January 1929*

Dr. Slipher and the
two other astronomers
put Clyde to work right away.
Clyde had many jobs.
He showed visitors
around the observatory.

After snowstorms, he climbed
onto the dome of the observatory
and pushed off the snow.
Clyde's most important job
was using the new telescope.
With it, Clyde would
take pictures of the night sky.
The astronomers were going
to use these pictures
to search for an unknown planet.

A man named Percival Lowell
had built the Lowell Observatory.
He believed that there was
a distant planet beyond Neptune.
He called it Planet X.
For many years,
Lowell searched for this planet.
He died in 1916, and Planet X
still had not been found.

Now the astronomers
at the Lowell Observatory
had the new camera telescope.
They also had a new machine
to help them compare
the pictures it took.
They felt sure they would
at last find Planet X.

Clyde used the telescope
each clear night to take a photo
of a part of the sky.
A few nights later,
he would take a photo
of the exact same part again.
The astronomers would then
compare the two photos.

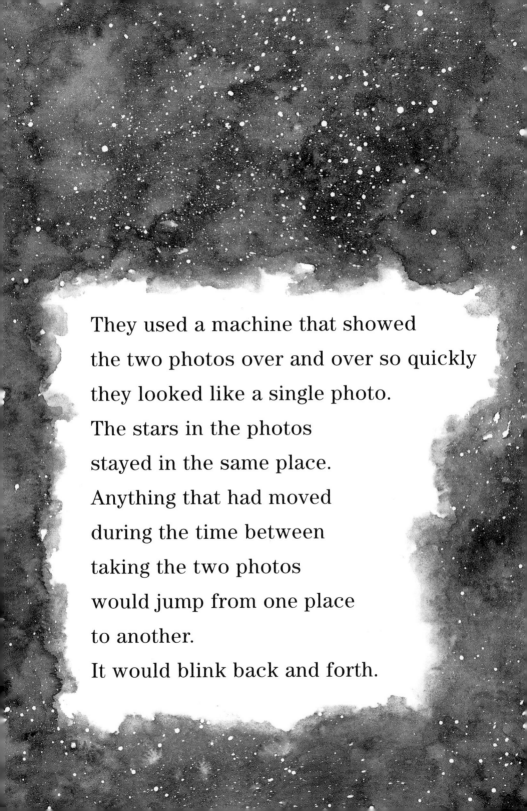

They used a machine that showed
the two photos over and over so quickly
they looked like a single photo.
The stars in the photos
stayed in the same place.
Anything that had moved
during the time between
taking the two photos
would jump from one place
to another.
It would blink back and forth.

Night after night,
Clyde spent long hours
in the cold telescope building
taking pictures of the starry sky.

Day after day,
the astronomers searched
for moving dots of light
on Clyde's photos.
Asteroids, comets, and planets
all orbit around the sun.
A moving dot of light
on the photos
might be an asteroid or a comet.
Or it might be Planet X.

Even with the machine,
searching the photos
was slow, hard work.
Months went by,
and the astronomers found
no sign of the planet.
They had other work to do.
Clyde's photos kept piling up,
but the astronomers stopped
looking at them.

In June, Dr. Slipher asked Clyde
to use the machine to search
the photos that he took.
Clyde could hardly believe it.
Dr. Slipher was turning over to him
the whole job of finding
—or not finding—Planet X.
Clyde was determined.
If Planet X was out there,
he would find it.

Clyde worked day and night
with very little rest.
At night, he used the telescope
to take pictures of the sky.
During the day,
he searched for moving dots of light
on his photos.
Each photo had tens of thousands of
tiny star images,
between 50,000 and 400,000
tiny dots of light.

Clyde made sure he checked
every inch of every photo.
He checked every single moving light.
He found many asteroids
and several comets,
but no Planet X.

More months passed.

Clyde began to wonder

if there really was

another planet out there.

Once, a visiting astronomer

told Clyde, "Young man,

I'm afraid you are wasting your time.

If there were any more planets

to be found, they would

have been found long before this."

After more than a year

at the observatory,

and eight months

searching all by himself,

Clyde still had not found Planet X.

But he kept on looking.

February 18, 1930,

was like any other day for Clyde.

He was looking at two photos

with the machine.

One had been taken on January 23,

the other on January 29.

He studied the photos

one small part at a time.

By four o'clock in the afternoon,

he still had not finished.

Then he saw it!

A tiny dot jumped back and forth.

He knew it wasn't an asteroid

or a comet because

the distance it jumped was too small.

Could this be Planet X?

Clyde got out a third photo,
one that he had taken on January 21.
With shaking hands,
he looked at the photo.
The dot of light was there,
exactly where he expected
it to be.
Now he was sure.

Clyde tried to look calm,
but his heart was pounding.
He walked down the hall
to the director's office.
"Dr. Slipher," said Clyde,
"I have found your Planet X."

Dr. Slipher and another astronomer
rushed to look at Clyde's photos.
They saw that it was true.
Clyde had found Planet X.
He was bursting with excitement.
But he could not tell anyone,
not even his parents, or Uncle Lee.
The astronomers wanted to take
more photos of the planet first.
They wanted to be absolutely sure.

On March 13, 1930,
the Lowell Observatory announced
the discovery of the ninth planet.
Planet X was named Pluto.
All around the world,
twenty-four-year-old Clyde Tombaugh
was a hero.
He had found a whole new world.
He had found Planet X,
hidden among the stars.

## Afterword

Actually, Pluto had been recorded in photos taken by Percival Lowell. Pluto was also in early photos that Dr. Slipher and others had examined. But those astronomers had all missed that tiny dot of light.

Dr. Clyde W. Tombaugh had a distinguished career as a world-renowned astronomer, writer, teacher, and inventor. Many of his inventions are used to track rockets in space. But it is Clyde, the twenty-four-year-old farm boy, spotting that faint image of Pluto, that has captured the hearts and imaginations of everyone interested in the stars.

## Important Dates

February 4, 1906—Clyde Tombaugh was born in Streator, Illinois.

August 1918—First looked through Uncle Lee's telescope

1922—Moved with family to Kansas

1925—Graduated from high school

1926—Made first telescope

1929—Started work at Lowell Observatory in Arizona

1930—Discovered Pluto (Planet X)

1932–36—Attended University of Kansas

1934—Married Patricia Irene Edson

1936–1943—Worked at Lowell Observatory

1939—Received master's degree from University of Kansas

1943–45—Taught celestial navigation for U.S. Navy

1946–1955—Developed systems for tracking rockets at White Sands, New Mexico

1958–1973—Taught as Professor of Astronomy at New Mexico State University

1960—Awarded honorary Doctor of Astronomy degree from Northern Arizona University

1979—Wrote *Out of the Darkness: The Planet Pluto* with Patrick Moore

1979–1997—Lectures, writes, observes

1997—Died on January 17